Coming Back to God When You Feel Empty:

Whispers of Restoration
from the Book of Ruth

Tanya Marlow

Coming Back to God When You Feel Empty:
Whispers of Restoration from the Book of Ruth

Cover image and design © Jon Marlow.
Used with permission.

All verses are taken from the NIV Bible. THE HOLY
BIBLE, NEW INTERNATIONAL VERSION®, NIV®
Copyright © 1973, 1978, 1984, 2011 by Biblica, Inc.™
Used by permission. All rights reserved worldwide.

For Rachel Lane, who first introduced me to (and caused
me to fall in love with) the book of Ruth,
and for Ruth Cooper, who is so like her namesake.

With many thanks to the amazing community at Thorns and
Gold, and all those who read, edited, and cheered me on in
the making of this book, including but not limited to
the crew at The Inkwell and Storytellers,
Master Marlow (whose suggested title was 'When Ruth
Gets Married')
and above all, to Jon.

What people are saying about *Coming Back to God When You Feel Empty*

"Tanya Marlow's wonderful reflections on the book of Ruth are rooted in life experiences. She shows how the story of Ruth still lives and resonates. If you are someone struggling with life, or you know someone who is and you want to know how to be a good friend for them, this will undoubtedly be a blessing to you."

Dr Jenni Williams,
author of *God Remembered Rachel: Women's Stories in the Old Testament and Why They Matter* and Tutor in Old Testament, Wycliffe Hall, Oxford University

"This is a book you can put into the hands of anyone who feels empty, disappointed, or hopeless. Marlow shows how God remains faithful today by sharing her own stories of loss, suffering, and faith alongside the narrative of Ruth. This book will leave you challenged and, most importantly, encouraged."

Ed Cyzewski,
author of *Coffeehouse Theology* and *A Christian Survival Guide*

"Intensely honest yet wonderfully gentle, Tanya's reflections on Ruth's story - and her own - provide both comfort and challenge to all of us seeking God in the midst of life's struggles. I recommend this little book to anyone who has ever doubted God, anyone who has been angry with him, anyone mired in exhaustion and despair - in short, anyone who is a Christian."

Dr Ros Clarke,
author and Discipleship and Training Pastor

Contents

Introduction

There are days when everything looks grey, your bones are weary, your heart heavy, and all you can see in your future is bleak and bland. There are days when you want to swear at the traffic, and slam every door. Every time there is an announcement in the news of another shooting or famine, you groan, and feel the helplessness of it all. You know somehow that you want to connect with God, but you don't know how, and you barely have the time or energy for it.

This book is for you.

If you have ever read the biblical book of Judges, then you will know that it is a bleak book, full of murder and sin; an ever-descending godless spiral. In happy contrast, set in the midst of the dark time of the Judges, we find the book of Ruth: a story of love and homecoming, an oasis of God's kindness.

Similarly, this short book is intended to be an oasis for anyone feeling empty or disappointed with God. I have often been the one who has felt empty or lost, and the book of Ruth has set me on a yellow-brick path back to God. It is filled with soft light and hope.

This book started life as a series on my blog, Thorns and Gold, and has been expanded and reworked. It gives a little snapshot of my story, intertwined with the story of Ruth, with some nuggets of gentle truth along the way.

The chapters broadly follow the chapters of Ruth, and at the end there are questions for reflection and a creative exercise.

Draw up an easy chair, pour yourself a cup of coffee; read, breathe and enjoy.

Chapter One: Stomping back to the Promised Land - Ruth 1

How do you respond when God has taken everything from you?

In 2010, I gained a baby, and lost the ability to walk more than twenty metres.

Myalgic Encephalomyelitis (ME) is a chronic, multi-system neurological illness, with no definitive cure; as well as the pain and plethora of symptoms that typically accompany it, it feels as though you are attempting to recover from a particularly evil strain of flu, like your body's battery is constantly flat. Though I had suffered from Myalgic Encephalomyelitis for several years, the exertion of labour pushed my illness into a more severe form of ME. Overnight, my legs and arms had no strength, and my concentration faded in a matter of minutes.

I had a gorgeous, pinkly new baby whom I was unable to lift. My world for the next eighteen months revolved around the spare bedroom, because it was next to the bathroom, and that was as far as I could walk. Once a fortnight, I saved enough energy to leave the house in a wheelchair for an hour in the sunshine, but it meant days of pain and exhaustion afterwards. I don't know much about economics, but considering the amount of energy I was saving, I didn't seem to be getting a good return on my investment. My existence had become numbingly, unremittingly beige.

Everyone, to varying degrees, experiences loss. (Anyone with contact lenses will know this all too well). Someone wise once said that "all change is experienced as loss", and even typically positive events like marriage and childbirth can bring with them their own sets of losses, alongside the gains. We gain a partner, but we lose the freedom to go where we please, and perhaps we have to sacrifice that job opportunity abroad. We gain a baby, but lose lie-ins and clothes that don't smell of baby sick. It is a positive change, but we still experience it as loss, and find ourselves inexplicably sad at the point where we expect to be most glad.

We move home, or church, or someone we love dies, or we get made redundant, or our health declines, or we age. As psychiatrist Harry Levinson has pointed out, "all change involves loss, and all loss must be mourned."[1]

It is now a few years on after the shattering of my world, and I have adjusted, even improved a little, though I still have to lie in bed for approximately twenty-one hours of the day. Most of the time I am content, but there are days when the loss hits me afresh, and I grieve the person I used to be. I recall the thrill of lecturing students in Biblical

---

[1] See further *Easing the Pain of Personal Loss*, Harry Levinson, Harvard Business Review, September-October 1972: Vol 50: No 5: page 80-88

Theology: that moment when all the faces in a room pause, and then collectively nod, and you know with a thud of satisfaction that your words have hit their target. I miss singing: proper operatic-style singing from The Marriage of Figaro, and soaring descants at Christmastime. Before I became ill I would run five miles, three times a week, and I remember with a pang the satisfying pulse and rhythm of trainers pounding on pavement.

Honest about emptiness

I am Naomi.

The book is titled after Ruth, but it begins with Naomi, and I do so like Naomi, because she is honest in her disappointments.

During the tumultuous and godless days when the Judges ruled Israel, there was a famine in the land, so Naomi and her husband decided to leave Israel and live in Moab, where the people worshipped foreign gods but had plenty of food.

Here is a girl who walks away from the place where God dwells because she is hungry, and tired of waiting. She is pragmatic, impatient. What was so great about a promised land if God wasn't looking after them? A girl has to eat.

So Naomi goes to live in a foreign land, and her sons marry people they're not meant to. Faithful Israelites were forbidden from marrying the Moabites, but who is she to argue with marrying Moabite women? It's not like they're living in Israel anymore. Believing in God is all well and good, but you've got to make do, you've got to survive somehow.

And then tragedy strikes, the days get darker: her husband dies. Her plans for self-preservation could not protected her from this loss. She grieves, and is comforted by her sons, and then - tragedy upon tragedy - both her sons die. Tragedy does not discriminate: it will revisit you even while you're still reeling from your first loss. She has no further close family in Moab to support her, so now she is vulnerable, living as a widow and foreigner in a land where her religion is despised.

What would you do if you were Naomi? Pragmatic as ever, she returns to her homeland of Israel, because it is the sensible choice, and her best chance of survival. She returns to God, but she is full of disappointment and grief.

"I went away full, but the Lord has brought me back empty," (Ruth 1:21a) she complains when she returns. Unlike many Christians today, she is not afraid to admit to the people of God her disappointment in God.

Stomping back to the Promised Land

Naomi returns home, but she does so reluctantly.

I ran away from home once, for about three hours. (Or perhaps thirty minutes - time passing is always hard to measure when you're a child). I stormed off down the road, turning down a country path towards the railway, just for half a mile or so, my hot tears cooling in the wind as I marched. When I was sure I was alone, I sat on a bank, and stared coldly at the sky, planning my future by myself, full of righteous indignation. The minutes ticked by: I pulled at the grass, and plucked seeds out of wild plants. The air grew chilly, the damp seeping into my clothes.

After a while, logic and sense overcame my anger, and I turned for home, because, really – what was I going to do? I was a child: I had no money, no car, and perhaps above all, no real inclination to make it on my own. I returned because I had to, but I slammed the door when I got in, and stomped my feet on the doormat to signal my displeasure.

(I am Naomi.)

"Don't call me Naomi," she says, as she comes back to face the equivalent of a massive school reunion. She is sulking. She will not be called by something that means 'pleasant'. It is a lie, and she does not want to pretend. "Call me Mara, because the Almighty has made my life very bitter." (Ruth 1:20)

Blessed are the grumpy

She is an old woman now, limping back to Israel because she has nothing left. She comes back because of the successful harvest, and perhaps the chance of finding financial support from distant family. As pragmatic as a child, she returns to God because she has to. She comes back to God and his land with stomping feet and a blackened heart.

When tragedy strikes and we are overcome with loss, some of us are Naomi. As Simon Peter points out, "Lord, to whom shall we go? You have the words of eternal life." (John 6:68). When my health crumbled, I turned to God, but with reluctance: stomping, slamming the door, railing at Him in my prayers. I was so very disappointed, and unable to understand why God had taken so much from me.

This is why I love that Naomi is featured so prominently in the Bible: it is a little nod from God that He knows our hearts, He dearly loves even the grumpy and overdramatic ones, and He includes us in His story. If you are feeling like Naomi did, empty and bitter, know that God loves you, and there is space for your disappointment and stomping.

The wisdom of craziness

As much as I love Naomi, it is Ruth's response that challenges me. In contrast to Naomi's pragmatism, even cynicism, Ruth's behaviour is foolhardy and illogical. Ruth is crazy for leaving Moab. Presumably she would have had relatives back at home who could have supported her.

As she stood with Orpah, her sister in law, and Naomi, her mother-in-law, at the edge of Moab, she had a choice to stay behind and do the sensible thing, or abandon all she had ever known in order to support an ageing widow. Of course, she too was a widow, and now in need of support herself. In Moab she would be vulnerable enough, but in Israel she would be even more ostracised: in a patriarchal society that valued women for childbearing, how would she survive, a childless widow and despised foreigner, speaking with a strange accent? It was lunacy to even consider the move.

But she went. Orpah was sensible, she loved her mother-in-law but she let her go. Ruth didn't just offer to accompany Naomi, she clung to her, physically holding onto her so that they would go on together. In committing to Israel, she wasn't only supporting her mother-in-law, she was changing her religion and turning to God. Perhaps she had seen something, even in heartbroken Naomi, of the goodness and truth of God, and she knew she had to follow Him.

She came to God's land as one who would trust the little she knew about Him. "Your God will be my God" – it is a simple, crazy confession of faith; no conditions, no ifs, no buts, no 'I'll see how it goes'; she jumped all in. It was utterly foolish - and utterly the right thing to do. She has the foolishness that is wiser than man's wisdom. She trusts God. She doesn't stomp, she clings.

Stomp like a child, or cling like a child

When some friends of mine lost their little baby, around the same time that I was facing my new-found disability, I watched them closely. Although I reserved for myself the right to be bitter in the face of suffering, I didn't want that for them. But though they wept, their grief was of a different order to mine: they clung to God in the darkness. They were Ruth, and they were as much of a challenge to me as they were a comfort. There is more than one way to respond to grief and emptiness.

❅ ❅ ❅ ❅

So what do you do when God has taken, and you're left with nothing?

Naomi stomps; Ruth clings.

I do not wish to condemn those who respond like Naomi and me, who are overcome with bitterness. I love her honesty, and the fact that the Bible records her honesty with such tenderness. Sometimes you just need to stomp, and even if you don't come with the right heart, you end up in the right place.

But Ruth's response calls to me. Perhaps, like me, you are learning, slowly, to respond like Ruth.

You want to come to God simply because you crazy-love him; you want to step into foreign lands when you have nothing, simply because you know His character. You want to go willingly to God, not because you are forced to.

Every once in a while, I want to shed the protective doubt. Even though I may look stupid, even if it seems crazy, I wish to choose to trust.

I am allowing myself to stomp; but I am learning to cling.

Read: Ruth 1

Over to you:

- When in your life have you felt empty, or faced loss?
- "All change (even positive change) is experienced as loss" - in which situations has that been true for you?
- What is your instinctive reaction when you face loss - to stomp, or cling?
- Which are you most like at the moment: Ruth or Naomi?
- What helps you to trust God in situations when life looks bleak?

Creative exercise:

Adopting a different posture while praying can be a powerful thing. The next time you are feeling frustrated or empty, perhaps try stomping while you pray. Then, try clinging - to a bed, maybe, or a pillow - imagining you are Ruth, clinging on to Naomi and to God.

- How does it feel to do this? What impact does this have on your prayers?

Chapter Two: Last-minute God - Ruth 1

With all the action in the first chapter of Ruth – the deaths and disasters and the beautiful friendship of Ruth and Naomi – this is a 'blink and you'll miss it' verse:

> "…the Lord had come to the aid of his people by providing food for them…" (Ruth 1:6)

As I look at that phrase, "the Lord had come to the aid of his people by providing food for them," a series of Biblical scenes flash through my mind:

- In the beginning, out of the nothingness and the void, God spoke colourful fruit onto every tree in Eden.
- In the desert, the dust intermingled with the bitterness of the Israelites' complaints: God heard them, and rained down manna, strange crackers they named 'wotsits', that were just enough to live on each day.
- The widow at Zarephath was preparing to die from hunger when a prophet asked her for something to eat. Her flour and oil miraculously continued to be renewed until the drought ended.
- When Jesus stood on green grass with a restless and hungry crowd, He multiplied a picnic lunch until five thousand people were stuffed full.

What does this tell us? God is the same, in the Old Testament, New Testament, and throughout the ages – the one who looks with compassion upon his hungry people and gives them good things. This was as true for the Israelites in Ruth's day: there was a famine, God heard them, and provided food for his hungry people.

God is aptly named by Abraham as Yahweh Yireh[2] (or "Jehovah Jireh", as it is often sung): He is the Lord who provides.

God's eleventh hour policy

God provides, true enough - but it feels so often that God is just a little late.

After all, God provided for his people and for Naomi and Ruth, sure – but look how long they had to wait! The crowd listening to Jesus were tired and hungry at the end of the day. The widow at Zarephath was about to die.

I find myself asking questions about God's scheduling. Why couldn't God do things just that little bit sooner? Why is his provision always so last-minute? (In short, why couldn't God be better organised, like I am?)

---

[2] See Gen 22:14

In the months after I gave birth, we limped along as a new family, and although Jon managed admirably: juggling work; taking our little boy to meetings; changing all the nappies; it was impossible for him to work full-time and look after our baby. We always hoped I would recover, but the weeks rolled by without improvement, and we had to face facts: we needed additional help.

As chance would have it, a good friend of ours was looking for gap year work. It didn't feel such a wrench handing over our precious bundle when we already knew and loved Lili, and we hoped this would buy us enough time for my health to improve.

After six months, when Lili had come to the end of her time with us, I still hadn't improved, and now we had no replacement childcare, just when our boy was starting to crawl and explore. We didn't want just anyone for our little boy, and we were so tired.

"God – why can't you just DO something?" I prayed, bleary-eyed. "Help us, please?"

It wasn't like we weren't doing 'our bit'. We were looking and making enquiries – but it was so hard to find someone trustworthy. We lost sleep. We kept making lists of possibilities, or hoping that, somehow, I would wake up and find myself better. And then, at the last minute, a few days before Lili left, we found a friend of a friend who could do it for a month. We breathed a sigh of relief.

"God has answered your prayers!" a friend exclaimed, and I wanted to explain that no, God hadn't answered them. Instead, He'd ignored us and we'd been frantic with worry until I had plundered my connections in various churches to find someone good. Naturally, I didn't say that, because it's not the Christian thing to do. I smiled, but I muttered under my breath to God:

"I gave you the credit for that one – you owe me."

❀ ❀ ❀ ❀

God provides food for his people – this is an unchanging truth.

But that doesn't mean that his followers are immune from ever feeling hungry.

For most disciples in the world today this is literally true. Saying grace before meals is never so meaningful as when you are living in a poor country with a poor family, your tummy is rumbling and you genuinely have no idea if there's going to be enough food for the next meal.

These things aren't simple. God is not a slot machine, a system to be worked out. People die of hunger every day in our world. Naomi and Elimelech were in Moab long enough for their sons to be married and then die, so the famine must have lasted a long time in Israel – had Israelites been dying of hunger in that time?

I wish that the book of Ruth dealt with those issues. But it doesn't. It simply wants to point us to the character of God, Yahweh Yireh, the Lord who provides.

The fingerprints of God

I reflected upon this in September 2012 when, once again, we were looking for a new nanny. I was remembering all the nannies we had come to know as friends over the preceding months – Lili, Sophie, Lizzie, Marie, Alyssa, Laura. As each one came into our house, our friends would marvel at how we had managed to get such a high calibre of nannies who were so reliable and loved our boy. We didn't know either.

Even when we had lots of notice, and could start looking and interviewing in good time, we never found anyone until right at the last minute. Each time, as I looked over the parapet of a following week with no childcare cover, Jon's diary full of important meetings and my body refusing to do more than stay in bed, I would say again in panic to God, "Help us! It's next week! We have no one to look after our baby! Can you not hear our prayers? Are you not getting this?"

But each time we would find a nanny, just as we needed them, just at the last minute. And not just any nanny, we would have amazing, better-than-Mary-Poppins-type nannies. It was almost as though there was a pattern.

I don't want to sound like I'm being super-spiritual here, and I always hesitate to give a supernatural reason when a natural one will do. But the fingerprints of God are all over Ruth's story when you stop to look, and maybe His fingerprints are over mine, too.

Maybe it was a coincidence of timing each time, but maybe it's that God was whispering to me that He is the God who provides for His people. (At the last minute.) Maybe he would provide for me again, as he did before.

That September, I did as I had before: recruited, phoned, interviewed, asked friends, but there was a crucial difference: this time I decided to trust that God would turn up.

And He did, with Izzy, our final and dearly-loved nanny. (At the last minute).

Sometimes it is good to be like Ruth, to look at the complexities of the situation, to feel the ambiguities, and then to trust in God's character anyway. He did it before, He'll do it again – it's in His nature.

So I say it aloud to the world with the shy-boldness of a child who is still learning to trust: God provides for his people.

And I dare to believe that whisper: God provides for me.

Read:

- Ruth 1
- See also Genesis 2:4-17, Exodus 16:1-5, 1 Kings 17:7-16, Matthew 14:13-21

Over to you:

- How easy do you find it to believe that God is Yahweh Yireh, the one who provides?
- What has been your experience of this?
- How do you feel when God's provision does not come until the last minute?

Creative exercise:

When we are worried about things, it can often help to identify them. On one side of a sheet of paper, write all the things you are most worried about in a big swirl, and on the other side, simply write "Yahweh Yireh", or perhaps an image of loaves and fishes.

- How does it feel to identify those worries?
- How does it feel to have that statement of God's provision proclaimed so boldly on the other side?

Chapter Three: Crazy stupid generosity - Ruth 2

It is hard for the rich to be generous.

This sounds counter-intuitive. Surely it's harder for the poor to be generous? When you have so many extra resources to spare, you can afford to be more generous than those who have little.

This is true, yet it's often the poor who are most generous. I noticed this in Africa.

When I was twenty, I joined a mission summer team, and helped to lead a church's Holiday Club for children in Zimbabwe. I knew the drill, because I had already run dozens of Holiday Clubs in Britain. Every day we played games, sang songs, taught the Bible, performed a drama, and watched the kids increase in excitement throughout the week. At the end of the morning, when they were getting restless, we led them in a craft activity, so that they had some tangible goods they could proudly present to their parents.

On this occasion, they baked cupcakes, and at the end, they offered some to us. We smiled at how polite they are, thanked them, told them it was theirs to enjoy, and they should take it home and eat it with their family.

In Britain, those children would have thanked us and taken all their cakes home. A really generous British child might have given us one of the six cakes, and we would have had tears in our eyes from how adorable they were.

These kids didn't play by the rules.

"No, no – really – have some," they said. They took the cupcakes and put them into our hands. They were distributing them liberally.

"Eat them, enjoy them."

We British leaders were confused.

"Don't you like them?" we asked.

They looked blankly at us.

"It's good to share," they replied.

I felt hollow. These were not rich children. We had taught them all that week that it was good to share – but that's just the thing you say to kids because you know they won't do it. It was a shock to discover that someone actually believed it.

We sat and ate with them. It was indeed good to share, and it did something peculiar to my heart.

Ruth is benefit-scrounging scum

There is a lot of noise from politicians today[3] about so-called 'strivers' (those who earn a wage) and 'skivers', (those in receipt of benefits from a welfare state). The rhetoric, so beloved of politicians looking to save some money, is that people who are out of work are a drain on the country; it is only those who are working and paying taxes who are respectable.

I had never realised the extent of the demonisation of those unlucky enough to have lost a job, or those too ill or disabled to work until I was the one claiming benefits. Filling out a form justifying why I was too ill to work felt like begging. I had always prided myself in my ability; now I had to focus on my disability. If you had told me as a teenager that I would be claiming benefits from the state for years, I would never have believed you: I had been a Grade A student, and in my twenties I carved out a career for myself in a field of work I loved.

Even as a teen, I used to say that I wouldn't like to win the lottery, because I believed in earning my money. (Now, however, I would not be entirely heartbroken if someone were to burden me with a million pounds: I would find a way to make my peace with it. Just in case anyone needs to know.) I posted off the form, cloaked in shame. Now I was

---

[3] For example,
http://www.theguardian.com/politics/2013/jan/09/skivers-v-strivers-argument-pollutes

one of 'them': a scrounger, a skiver, a beggar, scum, a drain on society.

Well, Ruth also was a skiver. That is not to say she was lazy - on the contrary, like most unemployed people today, (or those employed but on such a low wage they are in receipt of housing or tax benefit), she was hardworking and diligent, and worked all day to get her food. In this agrarian society, however, she would have been counted as a 'burden', and she was entirely dependent on handouts from those in power.

If you recall, Ruth had forsaken the security of her homeland to come to the Lord's country, because of her loyalty to Naomi and her God. She decided to work by gleaning (picking up the scraps from the harvest), and walked into that most miraculous of fields – one owned by someone who happens to be obeying God's law.

Boaz is J.K. Rowling

Boaz is a man of power and wealth; he has land, workers and respect. He could have abused his power so easily: turned Ruth away; even molested her, and there are clues in the chapter that other men would have done so without a second thought.

But Boaz is different. He greets his workers with 'The Lord bless you', and his actions show these words to be a prayer, not just something you say to check off the holiness box. He reveres God and takes His law seriously.

Moses said you were not allowed to super-efficiently harvest your fields for every last scrap, but only go over them once, leaving the bits at the edge for anyone to gather if they needed the food. Our tax system mimics this, though imperfectly: we are not to keep all of our profits but pay them to the state, and the welfare system ensures a percentage of taxpayers' earnings is distributed among the poor, sick and unemployed in our society.

Like our time[4], people were keen to get around these laws however they could. Who wants to pay their taxes? Boaz, however, was unusual.

Boaz was not a tax-avoider. In fact, remarkably, Boaz goes beyond this, telling the workers not to harm Ruth, sharing his own lunch with Ruth, instructing the workers to allow her to glean even among the good crop, and surreptitiously to pull out some stalks for her from the bundles.

J.K. Rowling, author of the phenomenally best-selling Harry Potter books, is a remarkable person: a multi-millionaire who pays her taxes without complaint.

---

[4] http://www.newstatesman.com/blogs/voices/2012/06/tax-avoidance-isnt-left-or-right-issue-its-cancer-eating-our-democracy

On the 14 April 2010, writing in The Times Online,[5] she said this:

> "I chose to remain a domiciled taxpayer for a couple of reasons. The main one was that I wanted my children to grow up where I grew up…
>
> "A second reason, however, was that I am indebted to the British welfare state; the very one that Mr Cameron would like to replace with charity handouts. When my life hit rock bottom, that safety net, threadbare though it had become under John Major's Government, was there to break the fall. I cannot help feeling, therefore, that it would have been contemptible to scarper for the West Indies at the first sniff of a seven-figure royalty cheque. This, if you like, is my notion of patriotism."

Boaz is not a tax-avoider; he is J.K. Rowling[6] – happily paying his taxes and giving money to charity above and beyond that.

Ruth comes home with so much barley that Naomi cannot believe it. Boaz doesn't just 'do his bit'. He is foolishly, imprudently generous, ridiculously so, just as

---

[5] See http://www.businessinsider.com/jk-rowling-on-high-taxes-2012-9?IR=T and
https://blogs.warwick.ac.uk/morleyd/entry/jk_rowling_the/
[6] http://www.takepart.com/article/2012/03/16/thankyoufriday-jk-rowling-no-longer-billionaire

Ruth was stupidly generous to follow her mother-in-law to a foreign country. They are a good match.

Boaz reflects Jesus

The Bible describes a God who fiercely loves the poor. Jesus urges Pharisees to be 'generous to the poor' (Luke 11:41), and he has choice words for teachers of the law who 'devour widows' houses' (Luke 20:47).

So too with Boaz - Boaz's heart beats with God's own love for the poor and the vulnerable. He doesn't make Ruth beg. He doesn't give her grain in return for turning a blind eye while his workers molest the foreigner, rather, he protects her. He goes out of his way to ensure she has more than enough.

And how does he interact with such a sponger? When Ruth comes to thank him, he doesn't bask in his glory as beneficent provider, modestly reflecting on how grateful he is that God has given him so much and how he can help those less fortunate. He doesn't shame her. In fact, he honours her. His focus is on God and on Ruth, not himself:

"Are you kidding? I'm the one who needs to be grateful. You have been amazing to Naomi, even leaving your homeland to look after her. You're the blessing, not me. I'm just so pleased you've taken that courageous step of coming to God – may you find shelter under his wings. Thank you.

I'm so grateful you're here and I pray that God will bless you abundantly." (Ruth 2:11-12 - somewhat paraphrased.)

Giving to the 'undeserving'

But who deserves such generosity? We need to be practical here. I come back with the arguments I read in the papers each day: we can't give to everyone. And what about those who have trapped themselves in poverty and just come begging? Surely we shouldn't have to give our hard-earned profits to them? Don't they need to first learn from their mistakes before we help them out?

In his excellent book, *Generous Justice*, Tim Keller points out that if we hesitate to give to those who seem 'undeserving' then we are hypocrites. God gave to us when we were undeserving. God's generosity will always far exceed our own. We don't make judgements, we just give generously.

We are generous – crazily, foolishly – because God has been crazily generous to us. This is our Trinitarian God: the Father who did not spare His own Son but gave Him for us all; the Son who was rich beyond all telling yet became poor so that we by his poverty might become rich; the Spirit who is poured out abundantly, generously on the church, who gives us gifts.

Crazy stupid generosity

Like Boaz, and like the Zimbabwean children who gave away all their cakes, this is how we should do justice: not patronisingly, but humbly and gladly, with hearts that echo God's generous heart. Boaz honours Ruth as an equal, not an object of his charity; as a woman, not as a project.

As a recipient of benefits, Boaz's actions console and validate me. But as someone who lives comfortably, and is, by global standards, exceedingly rich, Boaz's actions challenge me. The focus of his heart – on others and God – exposes my self-centred core.

It is harder for the rich to be generous.

Let's not just reserve one of our cakes to parcel out to the most deserving. Let's be foolishly, extravagantly generous.

I speak this to myself and I squirm as I see the hardness of my own heart, beating like a closed fist; shut tight like a padlocked treasure chest.

Read: Ruth 2

Over to you:

- How easy do you find it to be foolishly generous?
- Have you ever been in receipt of benefits or charity? How did it feel?
- What do you think about Tim Keller's contention that we should not worry about whether the recipient is 'deserving' or not, but to give without question or judgement?
- How can we give to others in a way that treats them as an equal, not as an inferior recipient of our charity?

Creative exercise:

- This month, give as generously as you are able, to anyone who asks. How does it feel to give indiscriminately?
- Additionally, ask someone to help you for something that you really need. How does it feel to be the one asking, the one in need?

Chapter Four: Against the grain - Ruth 3

When do you feel discouraged?

If you have ever found yourself waiting for something for a long time, with no change or improvement, it is easy to feel discouraged. In January 2013, I rang my ME doctor's secretary. It took a while to work up the nerve to ring, because I hated to make a fuss, but I didn't see any other option. When I walked to the bathroom, I had to cling onto the walls, dragging myself along slowly. My breathing was laboured just from being upright, and my heart was doing peculiar things. I had been given the all-clear by the emergency services that I wasn't about to drop dead, but that didn't stop my body behaving as though I was about to drop dead.

When I spoke to her, I explained that I hadn't seen my specialist for eighteen months, and I knew he was under-resourced and really busy, but, well, it had been eighteen months - could I please see him sometime soon, because I really was feeling quite unwell?

She paused while she went to look at my notes, and I held the phone to my ear as if I were holding onto a life preserver.

She came back on the phone, sounding sheepish: "I'm terribly sorry, but we seem to have lost your notes. We had a system change, and I think your file must have been archived. That's why no one has been in touch. The only way to get an appointment is to start the application again, and get put on the waiting list."

I tried to hold it together, but it was all too much. Right there on the phone, I sobbed.

The main thing running through my mind, apart from 'what do I do now?' was 'not again'. *Not again.* If you have ME, it is typically a struggle to be seen and taken seriously by doctors, and every day on my Twitter feed there are stories of ME patients who have been either neglected or abused by medical professionals. The whole system is broken, and I was just one of many falling through the cracks. I was disappointed, but a part of me had expected it.

I feel acutely the frustration of others, too - the marginalised in society who are ignored by those in power. Governments change, but justice doesn't come. History seems to repeats itself in a depressing cycle, and I feel powerless.

I write letters to my Member of Parliament, like I'm supposed to, and just get spin back. It feels like I am only one person, and I can't change the course of history.

I become desperate for things to change, and desperation is closely linked to despair.

Desperate for change

After crying, I figure that only thing I can do is to be savvy within the system; write letters, angry blog posts, use whatever power I have. I tell myself I need to play like they do: trickery, shortcuts, manipulation.

Again, I find myself as Naomi.

Naomi had gone to Moab when she was tired of waiting for food. Now Ruth was bringing home food, but she was still a widow, and Ruth marrying would be their best shot at financial security.

Naomi was tired of waiting for a husband to appear for Ruth: Boaz, though generous enough, had not shown any signs of proposing. She wanted a shortcut and she decided to make it happen.

She tells Ruth to dress seductively, to creep into a public place where she was not allowed, lie next to Boaz when he was asleep after eating (and drinking), and propose to him. Some think that Boaz's uncovered 'feet' actually refers to his genitalia. Whichever it was, it was a plan both audacious and risky, and it put Ruth in a very vulnerable position. Would Boaz take it as an honourable marriage proposal, or would he reject her as a harlot? What if he took advantage of her and raped her?

We think we know how the story will end. We know, because it is the exact same story we hear every week – the man shows no interest in getting married until his girlfriend gets pregnant and he's forced to reconsider his responsibilities. We know, because we have heard it before in the story of Tamar, Boaz's distant ancestor (Gen 38).

The same old story

Tamar's story is this: she is left as a vulnerable widow when her first husband, Er dies. However, there is a law that protects widows from permanent childlessness by obliging the dead husband's closest male relative, usually a brother, to marry the widow and give them children. The firstborn child of the new husband would be in the name of the deceased husband, to honour him and continue his line. This is known as Levirate marriage (based on the commands in Deuteronomy 25:5-10), and the new husband is known as the kinsman-redeemer or guardian-redeemer.

Onan, Er's brother, goes halfway to fulfilling his obligation. He marries Tamar but refuses to give her children; sleeping with her but spilling his semen on the ground so that she wouldn't get pregnant. God is not impressed by his attempts to cheat and deprive Tamar of children, so Onan dies too.

Judah, father of Onan and Er, grudgingly says that Tamar can marry his third son, Shelah, but only when he is older. So Tamar waits. Years go by. Shelah is finally old enough for Tamar to marry - but Judah reneges on his promise and Tamar can wait no longer.

She decides to take matters into her own hands. It is the same old story: injustice, the long wait, impatience, the shortcut.

She tricks her father-in-law, Judah himself into sleeping with her by disguising herself as a prostitute, and becomes pregnant by him. When Judah discovers she's pregnant he initially wants her burned to death for her immorality but his hypocrisy is exposed when he realises it is he who has made her pregnant. Guiltily, he admits that he hadn't done right by Tamar, and declares her to be more righteous than him.

The man who refuses to commit is tricked into doing what is right through the power of sex. It is an all-too familiar story, as much today as it was then.

One of the twins born to Tamar from her frustrated trickery of Judah is the great-great-great-great grandfather of Boaz, and our hearts sink as we envisage history repeating itself. We imagine the scene: Boaz using the alcohol as an excuse, Ruth with angry desperation saying it was too late and that she was pregnant; the resentment on both sides.

Against the grain

But - surprisingly, astonishingly - this doesn't happen.

When Ruth nervously pleads for Boaz's protection, "Spread the corner of your garment over me" (Ruth 3:9), Boaz doesn't take advantage of her, nor does he dismiss her for being immodest. He responds with humble gratitude that she has chosen him, an older man, explaining that the reason he didn't propose is there was a closer relative who is 'first in line' to opt to be Ruth's guardian-redeemer husband. He does not exploit Ruth, but neither does he attempt to shortcut God's law. He just wants to do the right thing.

Before she gets seen by the other men, he bestows on her a gift of grain, sending her back to Naomi with full hands and a hopeful heart.

Every now and again, I am reminded that there are a few good men in this world. If you will pardon the agricultural pun, Boaz goes against the grain.

- He goes against the grain of his wider family, who had a history of treating God's law very lightly.
- He goes against the grain of his society, which was ignoring God, everyone doing as they saw fit.
- He goes against the grain of his culture, which was to treat women as objects to be used and taken advantage of.

He honours God, and he honours Ruth. He lives as a person of integrity and kindness. And because of this, Boaz changes history.

When God cloaks you

I like to predict things. I research, I analyse. I study people and patterns of behaviour, and I protect myself from disappointment by anticipating the worst in people. We accept the sinful patterns of our family or wider society because, well, that's just always what happens; you have to be realistic. I see the trajectory of politics and society, and I laugh a hollow laugh because I saw it coming but felt powerless to change it.

And then, every so often, people surprise me. God surprises me.

A few days after my tearful outburst, when I had given up hope and numbly resigned myself to waiting months before seeing my specialist again, that same administrator rang me. She had been able to track down my notes from the archive, and in a few weeks' time I would have an appointment. She had compassion on my situation, and she had acted, like Boaz, with kindness. I wept again, this time in gratitude.

This gives me hope for the times when I am Naomi, powerless and scheming, sure that nothing will ever change. It gives me confidence for the times when I am Boaz, with an opportunity to be kind and compassionate, even if others are selfish. Sometimes the most unexpectedly powerful thing you can do is to be a person of integrity.

We don't know how many times God is working behind the scenes in people's hearts, and who knows - perhaps that last letter I send to my Member of Parliament may be a trigger for further action.

The righteous actions of just one person has the power to completely reverse the poison of several generations of sin. One person really can change the course of history.

And sometimes the vulnerable can plead to just one person, 'spread the corner of your garment over me', and find that it is God himself who cloaks them with protection.

Read: Ruth 3

Over to you:

- If you had been Ruth that day, how would you have felt? If you had been Boaz, how would you have felt?
- Which situations in your life feel like they will never change?
- What keeps you going when you feel powerless to change the system?
- Can you think of examples where one person's actions changed generations of sin?

Creative exercise:

- Read biographies of leaders like St Francis, Nelson Mandela, or others who changed the course of history by behaving righteously when others around them weren't.
- Write on a piece of paper all the situations that you feel desperate or despairing about. Keeping the paper nearby, wrap the warmest, cosiest cloak or dressing gown you own around yourself. Consider that God was working through Boaz to cloak with protection Ruth and, by extension, Naomi. Pray through what you are feeling.

Chapter Five: A life stitched with prayer - Ruth 4

I say it every night to my son, "May God bless you and keep you." Sometimes it is just as a reflex, a good habit to fall into so that my boy will have those words of God deeply etched into his soul. Sometimes I can barely hold back the emotion as I feel all of it for him – May God keep you safe. May you know Jesus and what the heart of life really is.

I pull the duvet up to him, tuck him in, stroke his head. He squirms and giggles under my touch. I want him to be covered over in love and safety. But I can't protect him. I can't watch over him. I am unbearably dependent on God to look after my son and hold him through the whiplashes of life.

Prayer: a mysterious tug of war

All of this I feel when I pray. The act of prayer is a mysterious tug of war: it simultaneously pulls him closer to me, towards my heart, whilst pushing him out into the hands of God.

Among the many ways I parent him, this seems one of the least significant. Feeding him helps him to grow – you can see it, measure it on charts and scales. Talking to him enhances his vocabulary – we hear it expand daily. We can record it, write it down. But prayer? He will not remember these prayers, there are no photos. There are just repeated words that daily float in the air.

And then I remember the book of Ruth and the prayers prayed; I recall the fingerprints of God, those little evidences of a spiritual world that creep through into the everyday.

May the Lord show you kindness

We had left Ruth waiting to see whether Boaz would marry her or whether the one who had 'first refusal' to be her guardian-redeemer husband would do it instead. The scene is in daytime, the whole village milling around to witness the business agreement. The closer relative is keen to get Elimelech's land, and agrees to be the guardian-redeemer. Alas - our love story is destroyed!

As the town collectively holds their breath, Boaz tells Ruth's relative that if he claims the land, he is duty-bound to marry Ruth, the widow, in order to preserve the name of the dead man with his property. It's not so attractive a business proposition if he has to take on the dead man's widow, because it might endanger his estate, so he declines the offer, and he removes his sandal to show he was relinquishing his right.[7]

---

[7] See Deut 25: 5-10. I'm glad to see that Ruth didn't spit in her relative's face. (Perhaps that's because he had already taken off his sandal.)

We exhale in relief, and Boaz marries Ruth. He doesn't need the money, he doesn't need the land, but he wants to obey God, honour his family, and protect and love this woman who has shown such kindness to Naomi.

Boaz shows Ruth kindness, and - voilá! - we have our happy ending.

But it all started with a prayer uttered by Naomi while she was still in Moab:

> "May the Lord show you kindness...May the Lord grant that each of you will find rest in the home of another husband." (Ruth 1:8-9)

God answered Naomi's prayer: He showed Ruth kindness, and she found rest in Boaz's home.

Blessings like confetti

It is fascinating to re-read the story of Ruth, highlighting all the prayers you find. When you start to look, there are prayers everywhere:

> "May the Lord deal with me, be it ever so severely, if even death separates you and me." (1:17)

This sounds like hyperbole from Ruth when Naomi is telling her to go back home to Moab, but she called on the name of the Lord to be her witness that she would not abandon Naomi. She took Him seriously, and she did not part from Naomi.

"The Lord be with you!" Boaz calls out to his workers, and "The Lord bless you!"(2:4) they reply as part of their daily greeting – and He was, and He did.

When Boaz meets Ruth in the harvest field and hears how she has committed to Naomi, he prays a blessing over her,

> "May the Lord repay you for what you have done. May you be richly rewarded by the Lord, the God of Israel, under whose wings you have come to take refuge." (2:12)

Boaz finds himself to be the answer to his own prayer: rewarding Ruth for her generosity to Naomi, covering Ruth with his protective garment of marriage, giving her refuge in his house and family.

When Ruth returns from gleaning and Naomi hears how Boaz has been generous to Ruth with the barley, Naomi prays for Boaz,

> "Blessed be the man who took notice of you...The Lord bless him!"(2:19, 20)

and by the end of the story Boaz is indeed blessed with a loving wife and baby boy, even in his old age.

"The Lord bless you, my daughter," (3:10) prays Boaz in gratitude over Ruth, even as she asks him to marry her.

At the wedding the whole town is involved, and prayers erupt from them in a symphony of blessing, falling like confetti over the newly-married couple.

For Ruth they pray that she will be like the heroines of the family she has just entered into – Rachel, Leah, Tamar. They pray that God will be faithful to her as He was to them:

> "May the Lord make the woman who is coming into your home like Rachel and Leah, who together built up the family of Israel. May you have standing in Ephrathah and be famous in Bethlehem. Through the offspring the Lord gives you by this young woman, may your family be like that of Perez, whom Tamar bore to Judah." (4:11b-12)

And the final prayer of the book is a blessing for Naomi:

> "Praise be to the Lord, who this day has not left you without a guardian-redeemer. May he become famous throughout Israel!" (4:14-15)

God answered those prayers. Ruth and Boaz did indeed build up the family of Israel, and they became famous in Bethlehem and Israel - and indeed the whole universe: they were the great-grandparents of the great King David and therefore ancestors of the greatest King to come. They were blessed.

And so too was Naomi, who had not been abandoned as she had thought when she left Moab, but was now provided for, with a loyal daughter-in-law, a rich guardian-redeemer son-in-law, and a bouncy baby grandson.

A life stitched with prayer

We don't notice the prayers as we read the story, but when we search for them, they are everywhere, stitched into the rhythm of their everyday life and language.

The book is called Ruth, but it starts and ends with Naomi. Naomi is the secret heroine, the undeserving sinner who is confused and bitter, who schemes and manipulates – and whom God blesses anyway. No longer called Mara, the bitter one, Naomi ends her days as her name suggests, pleasantly, with a wedding and a grandson.

It starts with the loss of sons, and ends with the women of the village shouting, 'Naomi has a son!'

It starts with a famine, and ends with an abundance of grain.

It starts with bitterness, and ends with blessing.

And throughout it all there are the prayers, these simple requests from people who trusted in a generous God.

As I stroke my boy's fair hair, still damp from his bath, I recall again the abundance of the grace of God, His undeserved love, the holy hands that pour blessing into my lap when I least expect it. I look into my little boy's eyes, full of trust and light. I remember, I remember that God answers prayers. I want to offer up words of supplication, however puny; I want to have a life stitched together by prayer.

I pray these words for my son, I pray them for me, I pray them for you:

May you be like your godly forebears.
May you be part of something bigger than your life.

May you be like Ruth,
the courageous one,
who loves abundantly and clings to God.

May you be like Boaz,
a person of integrity,
obeying God's law even in the secret places.

May you be like Naomi,
loved despite your failings and hurts,
overwhelmed by God's unexpected blessing.

May you know God the provider,
who feeds his people.

May you know Jesus,
who loved you and redeemed you,
and took you to be his wife,
even when you were a poor foreigner,
helpless and dependent.

May you know the whisper of the Spirit
as He directs your life
in ways that you are barely aware of.

May you know God the Trinity,
who reverses all our expectations,
who raises up the poor and vulnerable,
whose ways are not our ways,
and who gives us grace upon grace.

May the fingerprints of God be all over your life,
may his authorship be evident in your story.
Amen and amen.

Read: Ruth 4, and the prayers in Ruth

Over to you:

- How often do you pray prayers of blessing for yourself or others? Why is this?
- How can you incorporate prayer into the natural rhythms of your life?
- Have you ever seen the answer to many generations of prayer for the same thing?
- Which, if any, written prayers of blessing do you like to pray?

Creative exercise:

- Take a photograph of someone you love, and as you look at them, choose one or two lines of the blessing above to pray over them.
- Take a cup of rice, and pour it slowly into your lap, envisioning the blessings that God gives as rich grain. Take the time to run your hands through the rice as you pray the prayers of blessing for yourself. How does it feel? What are some of the rich blessings God has poured into your lap?

Author's Note

Thank you very much for reading Coming Back to God When You Feel Empty: Whispers of Restoration from the Book of Ruth. I would love this to be a resource for as many people as possible, so if you enjoyed it, I would be very grateful if you could spread the word to others by pointing them to my website or wherever you purchased it.

If you could leave a review on Amazon, or your preferred review site, that would also be an enormous help.

If you haven't already, please do sign up on my website to receive my free newsletter, which contains the latest book news, exclusive updates and offers, conveniently in your inbox a few times a year.

Please stop by and let me know what you thought of it, and a little about you - I'd love to know. I would love to connect with you further: I am on Twitter @Tanya_Marlow and you can find out more of my story at my website, tanyamarlow.com.

Thank you.

More praise for *Coming Back to God When You Feel Empty*

"A book which emerges from the muscle and gristle and grind of life rather than merely portraying it will always offer us more as we read. This is such a book. Tanya's writing is visceral and searingly honest. Her approach is essential to our struggle to make any kind of sense of suffering, not least in the light of the lives of biblical characters."

Wendy Bray,
award-winning author of *In the Palm of God's Hand*
and other books

"The narrative, which moves backwards and forwards between Tanya's story and the book of Ruth, takes us from darkness to light, from despair to hope, and from doubt to certainty. By the end I found myself wanting to read it again more slowly, and to sit with the very helpful questions and challenges at the end of each chapter."

Matthew Caminer,
author: *A Clergy Husband's Survival Guide* (SPCK 2012)
and *Curacies and How to Survive Them* (SPCK April 2015)

"Tanya Marlow provides an invitation to linger in the book of Ruth, tells us her own moving story, and brings both to intertwine with our own lives."

Cara Strickland,
writer

"Tanya Marlow's graceful and grace-filled insights into the book of Ruth kept my attention throughout my first insatiable reading, and call me back again and again for new nuggets of wisdom, hope, and gratitude. Her gentle but penetrating words are most welcome in a world full of surface living and attention-getters."

Jenn LeBow,
writer

"An inspiring read and a book to turn to when you feel you are ebbing. There is so much to learn from this enlightening work."

Aimee Coelho,
teacher

"The way Tanya Marlow writes about Ruth and Naomi, interspersing them with stories of her own life, brings them to life and puts flesh on them, reminding us they were human just as we are."

Gayl Wright,
writer

"*Coming Back to God When You Feel Empty* takes on injustice and chronic illness with grace and a whisper, "God provides for me." It inspires me to do the same when I forget how very true that is."

Lana Phillips,
seeker and storyteller

For further reading at
Thorns and Gold

If you liked this, you'll like these. You can find blog posts on *Thorns and Gold* which are related to each chapter linked here: http://tanyamarlow.com/relatedposts-comingback or by using the individual links below.

Stomping back to the Promised Land:

- Running Away From God
  http://j.mp/stompingback1
- Learning to Trust http://j.mp/stompingback2
- God is Not Sensible http://j.mp/stompingback3
- On Bidding Goodbye to a Difficult Year
  http://j.mp/stompingback4

Last-minute God:

- When God's love language is serving
  http://j.mp/lastminutegod1

Crazy stupid generosity:

- This should not be http://j.mp/crazygenerosity1
- Why this government is failing the disabled AND
  the taxpayer (DLA vs PIP)
  http://j.mp/crazygenerosity2

Against the grain:

- On the occasion of my MP coming to visit me
  http://j.mp/againstthegrain1

A life stitched with prayer:

- Living in the desert (A Praying Life)
  http://j.mp/lifestitchedwithprayer1

Tanya Marlow

Tanya Marlow was in Christian ministry for a decade, and a lecturer in Biblical Theology. She is now housebound with severe ME, and maintains a writing ministry from her bed.

She loves answering the tricky questions of faith that most avoid, and writing honestly about suffering and searching for God.

She is married to a vicar, but is terrible at flower arranging and quiche-baking, and they live in South-West England with their son and a collection of dying pot plants.

Tanya blogs at tanyamarlow.com